More Dubliners Songs.

Exclusive distributors:
Hal Leonard,
7777 West Bluemound Road, Milwaukee, WI 53213
Email: info@halleonard.com

Hal Leonard Europe Limited,
42 Wigmore Street Marylebone, London, WIU 2 RY
Email: info@halleonardeurope.com

Hal Leonard Australia Pty. Ltd.
4 Lentara Court Cheltenham, Victoria 9132, Australia
Email: info@halleonard.com.au

Order No. AM23078
ISBN 978-0-86001-581-9
This book © Copyright 1979 Hal Leonard

CONTENTS

4 INTRODUCTION

0 THE SPANISH LADY

2 KILLIEBURN BRAES

4 PLOUGHBOY LADS

6 RAGLAN ROAD

8 MATT HYLAND

21 THE BANKS OF THE SWEET PRIMROSES

22 SPANCIL HILL

24 PARCEL OF ROGUES

26 CARRICKFERGUS

28 BUNCLODY

30 SEVEN DRUNKEN NIGHTS

32 THE LARK IN THE MORNING

34 THE ENNISKILLEN DRAGOON

36 THE RISING OF THE MOON

38 AVONDALE

41 THE UNQUIET GRAVE

42 KELLY THE BOY FROM KILLAN

44 FOUR GREEN FIELDS

46 THE TOWN I LOVED SO WELL

48 FALSE-HEARTED LOVER

INTRODUCTION

The songs which have been selected for this, the second Dubliners Songbook, cover the broad spectrum of both folk song in general and the Dubliners repertoire in particular. This is especially so when they are taken in conjunction with the volume which has gone before. Ah, but what is folk song? you may ask. What indeed.

The libraries of the world doubtless contain volumes which explore the subject at great length and inceed the subject is one well worth the exploration. To put it at its simplest folk song must, of necessity, have been the popular music of its day, for amongst a population which was largely unlettered, oral transmission of song, music and lore would have been the rule rather than the exception. The songs usually fall into five or six distinct categories; love, seduction, nonsense, emigration, as well as protests against injustice and rallying cries during the periods of mass unrest, if not downright rebellion, which to the present day is writing Irish history in blood.

That doesn't of course mean that a 'life is real, life is earnest' atmosphere pervades the average Dubliners concert. In fact quite the contrary, Whether one is listening spellbound to Luke Kelly singing **Raglan Road** or Jim McCann singing **Carrickfergus**, or deflating the man or woman from **Rent-A-Heckler Ltd**. with remarks like "I don't know what he's drinking but I can recommend it to the rest of you", from the outset most of the audience are **In Their Granny's**. The latter is the Dublin vernacular for having a great time.

Some of the songs keep alive events in history and the men and women who were part of them. **Kelly The Boy From Killan** and **The Rising Of The Moon** date from the time of the 1798 Rebellion. For months before-hand pikes were forged in secret and men drilled and trained in remote areas. For a time it looked as if the rebels, ill-equipped as they were to face the artillery and professional soldiers, might just triumph. This was especially true in the wexford area where they were led by John Kelly from Killan, Fr. John Murphy and Bagnal Harvey. It is a common misconception that the rebels were invariably Irish peasant Catholics. Certainly with regard to this rebellion this was far from the case. The most respected of the leaders, apart from those just mentioned, were Theobald wolfe Tone, Thomas Addis Emmet, and Lord Edward Fitzgerald of the Geraldine Clan (dubbed the **Beloved Geraldine** by the plain people of Ireland) and the brother of the then Duke of Leinster . All were Protestant and all believed passionately in the right of the Irish people to govern themselves. Ironically it was this rebellion, or rather the acts of coercion with which it was put down which led directly to the ending of the so-called Grattan's parliament (in which the Duke of Wellington sat at one time) and the Act of Union in 1801. All of the leaders mentioned, with the exception of Emmet who went to America, died violently and, to the Irish may of thinking, shamefully. These men caught the public imagination and their heroism in the face of great odds lived on to inspire generations to come.

Charles Stewart Parnell who inherited the Avondale Estate was another such popular hero, nearer to our own time. His love affair with Kitty O'Shea, a married woman, scandalised Victorian Society. One cannot help but see the hands of political opportunists in his eventual downfall for he had been living openly with the lady for the best part of ten years before political expediency dictated that he should be publicly disgraced. Yet another Home Rule Bill was thrown out as a result and the hopes of the common people of Ireland were dashed yet again. Captain O'Shea divorced his wife and in due course Kitty and Parnell were married. A week or so later Parnell was dead - of a broken heart many said. **Avondale's Proud Eagle** though has not been forgotten for not only is there a street named after him in the centre of Dublin, there is also a magnificent monument to him at the top of O'Connell Street (Dublin's main thoroughfare), when Nelson's Pillar was blown to smithereens in March 1966 it was said by some wags (a breed which proliferates in Dublin) that this now put Parnell on a higher station.

Parcel Of Rogues was of course written by Robbie Burns, Scotland's national poet. It effectively shows what anger and disgust was felt in that country too, not so much against foreign rule, which was of course part of it, but against the political jobbers and time-servers, the traitors and knaves who sold their own people in return for

money, position, or power or all three.

The Scots and the Irish have seen, for the most part anyway, uprisings as the only way out of their difficulties, whereas the English working classes - who were every bit as oppressed as their fellows to the north and west - used other means to get what they wanted.

The whole picture is brought up to date with Tommy Makem's **Four Green Fields** and Phil Coulter's **The Town I Loved So Well**. Both the writers are Ulstermen. Tommy, the son of Sarah Makem, renouned for her traditional singing, was born and reared in Keady in County Armagh while Phil Coulter, internationally famous as co-writer of such songs as **Puppet On A String** and **Congratulations**, is a native of Derry - the town he loved so well. Tommy's song goes further back into history than Phil's but both express the writer's deep concern for what is happening in Ireland as well as their hopes for the future.

It has long been assumed that the national disease in Ireland is alcoholism. Granted drinking has been a major problem for centuries. To my mind though the bane of Irish life is, and always has been, emigration. While some went to join foreign armies and thereby perhaps gain the chance to have a crack at the hated English, most Irish people left home in search of a better life for themselves and their families. That being, so our folkmusic is liberally laced with songs of emigration. Jim is wont to introduce the song **Spancil Hill** with a flippant "Instant homesickness, just add Guinness" then add reflectively "I've even known it happen on the Isle of Man Ferry". Remarks like that are not intended to wound. They are simply a way of emphasising that in that particular context Entertainment is the name of the game.

In **Spancil Hill** the young man is dreaming of the home and the people he left behind him while in **Bunclody** the young man is thinking of emigrating because the young lady he'd set his heart on wants nothing to do with him because of his lack of material wealth. This latter situation was an all too common one in the social history of these islands. These days it is very difficult for us to comprehend the social pressures which were brought to bear on women particularly to marry money, or position.

Again folk song is rife with broken token songs when a young man comes home after a number of years abroad and tests his sweetheart's fidelity by pretendinq to be someone else and saying that her lover has died. There was no Women's Liberation Movement in those days - any young man who tried that one would be sent away with the proverbial flea in his ear.

Jim McCann publicly states that the song **Killieburn Braes** proves without any doubt that the women are worse than the men, with a grin he will often say as much from the stage to annoy any women's Libbers in the audience. On one occasion there was a comeback. This was in the Fairfield Hall in Croydon. When Jim asked if there were any women's libbers in the audience I Quickly replied "Yes. Me". With comic amazement he came back with "Since when?" "I've just joined!" - I very nearly did too.

The **Spanish Lady** is another nonsense song in this sense, Despite its title it is in fact native to Dublin and in the fifth verse the singer takes his listeners on a mini, verbal tour of the city, Three of the references have great historical significance; Patrick's close,

The Gloucester Diamond and Napper Tandy's House. The first is in the heart of the Liberties, the oldest part of the city and the place where all true Dubliners are said to be born. It is the close of St. Patrick's Cathedral, whose most famous incumbent was of course Dean Swift, who over the years became very bitter about his lack of preferment. Fortunately, as far as the world of literature is concerned this in no way prevented him from adding such classics as **Gulliver's Travels** to the world's riches.

The Gloucester Diamond has also gone douwn in history as James Joyce's **Nightown.** It is not something of which we are particularly proud but at one time that area was one of the most notorious Red Light Districts in Europe.

Napper Tandy was a political activist, and thorn in the side of the Establishment during the latter half of the eighteenth century. Despite his many run-ins with authority he died in his bed of natural causes.

Ireland is not noticeably to the fore in the world's Greatest Lover stakes. As Jim, again, has been heard to remark when introducing the song **Matt Hyland** on stage; "You can tell he's an Irishman. He has this beautiful girl in his bedroom for half an hour and all they do is hold hands!" That is not to say that we don't have some beautiful love songs. One would have to go a long day's march before being able to match the beauty of **Carrickfergus**, **The Enniskillen Dragoon,** or the contemporary **Raglan Road**. The latter was written by Patrick Kavanagh, the poet. It is said that he wrote this very beautlful song for a student with whom he fell in love - a love completely unrequited. Set to the

traditional tune **The Dawning Of The Day** the song has a haunting beauty which lingers long after hearing Luke sing it in concert.

While these songs are very Irish in feel and sound, songs like **False-Hearted Lover, The Banks Of The Sweet Primroses** and **The Unquiet Grave**, even when performed in the inimitable style of the Dubliners have definite English overtones. By the very nature of things where people travel song will too, and thankfully ethnic origins do not preclude one from either singing a song nor yet from enjoying it and perhaps draining a measure of intellectual stimulation from it.

The folk purists are, to this day, arguing about the origins of **Seven Drunken Nights** which took the Dubliners into the Pop Charts more than ten years ago. Seamus Heaney who gave it to them always insisted that the song concerned, not an unfaithful wife but in fact a man

who on returning home after some twenty years roaming the world in search of fame and fortune (the time honoured emigration theme again) finds a fully-grown son, whose existence he'd never even suspected, sharing the family bed. Even the most cursory study of social history will show that is not in the least far-fetched. The song sold in its thousands, mainly because folk hoped that the other two nights of the week would be mentioned. They weren't.

Songs of seduction are common to most folk traditions. Tommy Makem summed it up very succinctly recently when he said that women sow their wild oats during the week and then go to church on Sunday to pray for a crop failure. The universal theme of songs like **Ploughboy Lads**, or **The Lark In The Morning**, (or as Jim will have it "a bird in the forenoon"), is boy meets girl, teaches her more than her prayers, then takes off and leaves her first to talk her way round her pregnancy and then with a baby to dandle on her knee.

How many times has one heard the phrase "It's all part of life's rich pattern" uttered with wry humour and a sense of irony. I can recall any number. But in fact there is a rich pattern to living with many colours and facets and not a few surprises. It is our hope that with this present selection of songs from the Dubliners repertoire at least a little of that rich pattern is reproduced for your interest and pleasure.

The job of compiling this book was made easier for me thanks to the help of my friends the Dubliners, Jack MacGowan, Kevin O'Connor, Mel Macleod and Ken Stewart who, as we would say in Dublin, "held my hand till the tram passed."

Mary Hardy
23 March 1978

THE SPANISH LADY

Traditional
This arrangement (c) Copyright 1978 Tolka Music

I went out through Dub-lin Ci-ty at the hour of
I came back through Dub-lin Ci-ty at the time of
I went round old Dub-lin Ci-ty when the sun be-
stopped to look but the watch-man passed says he "young fel-la now the
I went out through Dub-lin Ci-ty as the hour of
wan-dered north and I've wan-dered south through Sto-ney-batter and

twelve in the night, Who should I see but the Spa-nish La - dy
half past eight, Who should I see but the Spa-nish La - dy
- gan to set, Who should I meet but the Spa-nish La - dy
night is late, A - long with you now or ____ I will wres-tle you
dawn was o'er, Who should I see but the Spa-nish La - dy
Pat - rick's Close, Up and a - round by the Glou-cester Dia - mond

[6th time ⌒ Rubato]

Wash-ing her feet by can - dle - light. First she washed ___ them
Brush-ing her hair so trim and neat. First she teased ___ it
catch-ing of moths in a gol - den net. When she spied ___ me
Straight - way through the Bride-well Gate." I blew a kiss ___ to the
I was lone - ly and foot - sore. First she coaxed ___ me
round by Nap - per Tan - dy's house. Old age had laid ___ her

KILLIEBURN BRAES

Traditional
This arrangement (c) Copyright 1978 Tolka Music

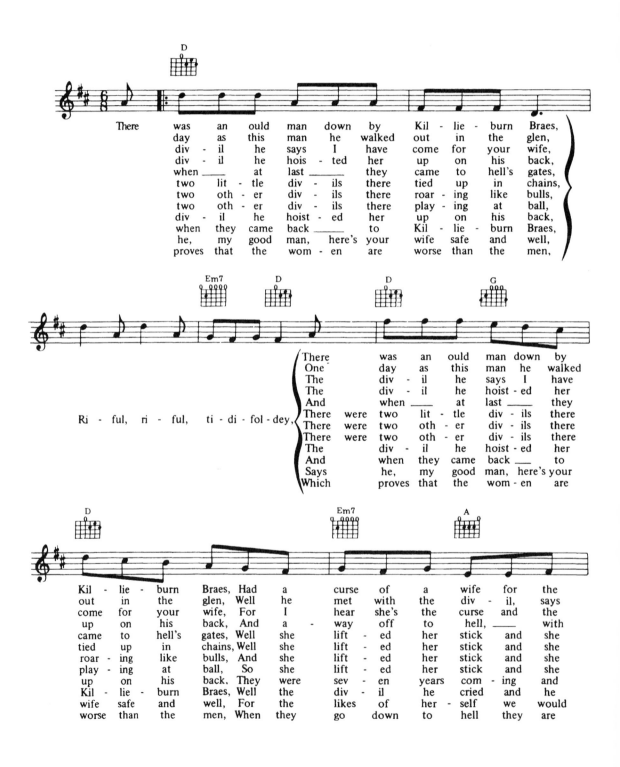

most   of   his   days,
how   are   ye   then.
bane   of   your life.
her   he   did   whack.
batt - ered his pate.
scatt - ered their brains.
batt - ered their skulls.
batt - ered them all.
days   go - ing   back.
shout - ed hoo - ray.
not   have in   hell.
thrown   out a -   gain.

With me ri - ful dol - dol,   'ti - di fol - lol,

Fol - a - dol - dol,   da   dol - da - dol - dey.

2.   One
3.   The
4.   So the
5.   And
6.   There were
7.   There were
8.   There were
9.   So the
10. And
11. Says
12. Which

Last time

To Fade

13

PLOUGHBOY LADS

Traditional
This arrangement (c) Copyright 1978 Tolka Music

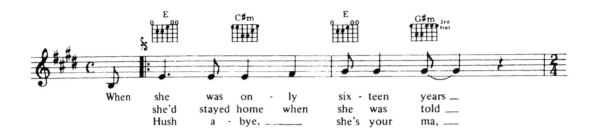

When she was on - ly six - teen years __
she'd stayed home when she was told __
Hush a - bye, _____ she's your ma, __

A beau - ty she __ was wear - ing, Ah
And done her mam - my's bid - den, oh, She
But the Lord knows who's __ your dad - dy oh, So

lit - tle lit - tle __ did she think __ that she'd be soon a -
not be sit - ting by yon fire - side __ singin' hush - a - bye my
maids take care and __ ye be - ware __ of the young man in the

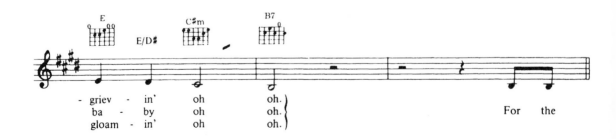

- griev - in' oh oh.)
ba - by oh oh.)
gloam - in' oh oh.)

For the

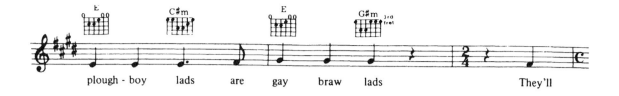

plough - boy lads are gay braw lads They'll

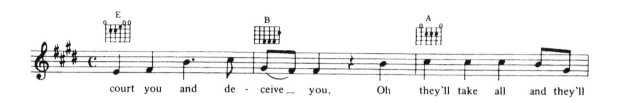

court you and de - ceive __ you, Oh they'll take all and they'll

gang a - wa' __ And leave the las - ses griev - in', oh

To Coda ⊕ 1 2 *D.S. al Coda*

oh. 2. If

⊕ *CODA*

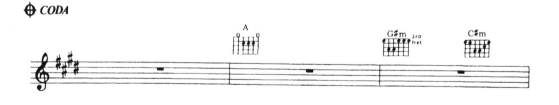

RAGLAN ROAD

Words and music by Patrick Kavanagh
(c) Copyright 1978 Katherine B Kavanagh

On ___ Rag - lan Road ___ of an
Graf - ton Street ___ in Nov -
gave ___ her gifts ___ of the
qui - et street ___ where

aut - umn day ___ I ___ saw her ___
- em - ber we ___ tripped ___ light - ly a -
mind ___ I gave her the ___
old ghosts meet ___ I see her ___

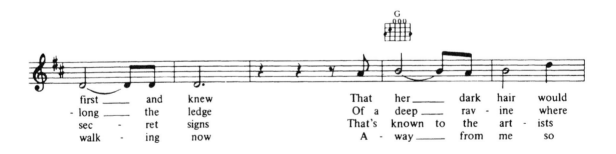

first ___ and knew That her ___ dark hair would
- long ___ the ledge Of a deep ___ rav - ine where
sec - ret signs That's known to the art - ists
walk - ing now A - way ___ from me so

weave a ___ snare that ___ I might one day
can be ___ seen the ___ worth of pass - ion's
who have ___ known the true gods of sound and
hur - ried - ly my ___ reas - on must al -

MATT HYLAND

Traditional
This arrangement (c) Copyright 1978 Tolka Music

There ___ was a lord who lived in this ___
straight a - way to her love she ___
both sat down up - on the ___
lord dis - coursed with his daugh -ter ___

town Who had a love - ly hand - some daugh -
goes In - to his room to a - wake ___
bed Just for the side of one half ho -
fair One night a - lone in her cham -

- ter. She was court - ed by a ___
him. Saying a - rise my love and ___
- ur. And ___ not a word by ___
- ber. Saying we'll give you leave for to

fine young ___ man Who was a ser - vant to her
go a - way This ver - y night you will be
eith - er ___ said As down their cheeks the tears did
bring him ___ back Since there's no one can win your

THE BANKS OF THE SWEET PRIMROSES

Traditional
This arrangement (c) Copyright 1978 Tolka Music

SPANCIL HILL

Traditional
This arrangement (c) Copyright 1978 Tolka Music

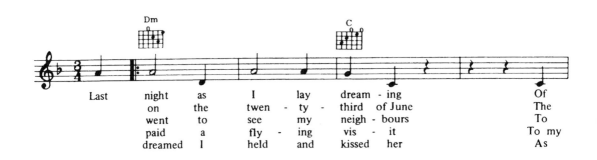

Last	night	as	I	lay	dream - ing		Of
	on	the	twen -	ty -	third	of June	The
	went	to	see	my	neigh -	bours	To
	paid	a	fly -	ing	vis -	it	To my
	dreamed	I	held	and	kissed	her	As

plea	- sant	days	gone	by,		My	mind	then
day		be -	fore	the	fair,	When	Ire -	land's
see		what	they	might	say,	The	old	ones
first		and	on -	ly	love,	She's	as white	as
in		the	days	of	yore,	Ah	Johnny	you're

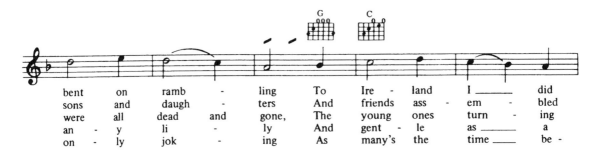

bent	on	ramb	-	ling	To	Ire -	land	I	did
sons	and	daugh	-	ters	And	friends	ass -	em -	bled
were	all	dead	and	gone,	The	young	ones	turn -	ing
an -	y	li -		ly	And	gent -	le	as	a
on -	ly	jok	-	ing	As	many's	the	time	be -

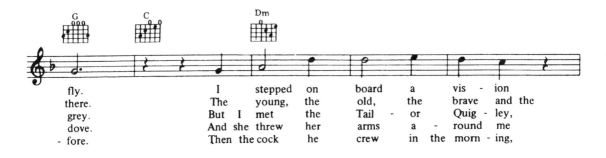

fly.		I	stepped	on	board	a	vis -	ion
there.		The	young,	the	old,	the	brave	and the
grey.		But I	met	the	Tail -	or	Quig -	ley,
dove.		And she threw	her	arms	a -	round	me
- fore.		Then the cock	he	crew	in the	morn -	ing,

22

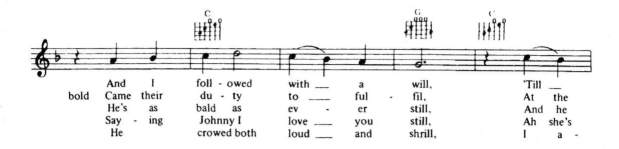
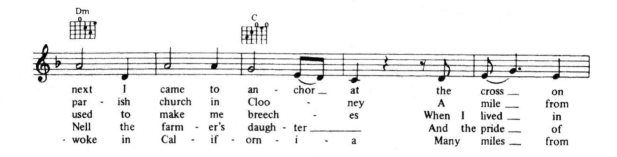
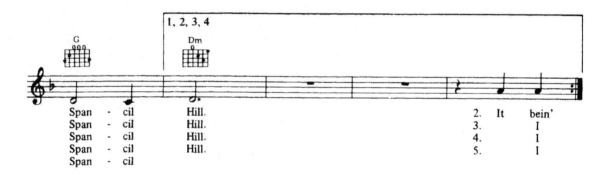
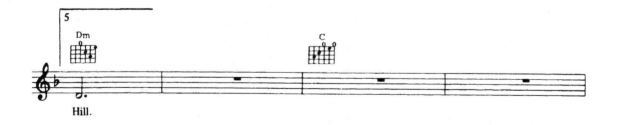
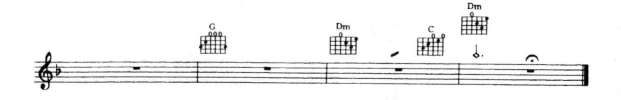

PARCEL OF ROGUES

Traditional
This arrangement (c) Copyright 1978 Tolka Music

CARRICKFERGUS

Traditional
This arrangement (c) Copyright 1978 Tolka Music

BUNCLODY

Traditional
This arrangement (c) Copyright 1978 Tolka Music

SEVEN DRUNKEN NIGHTS

Traditional
This arrangement (c) Copyright 1978 Tolka Music

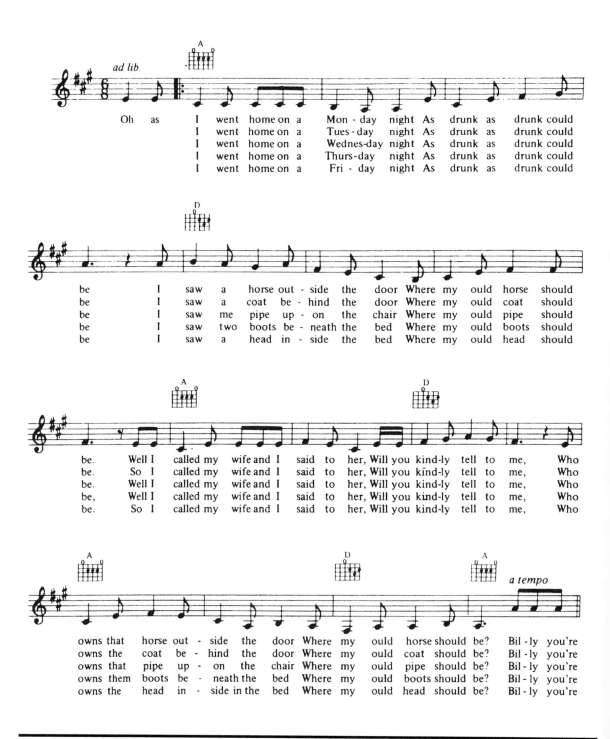

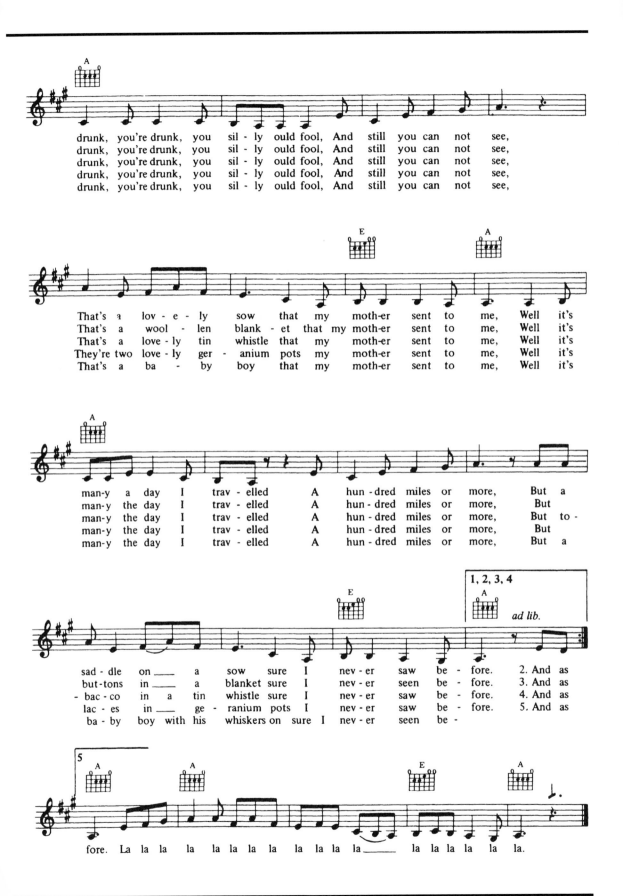

THE LARK IN THE MORNING

Traditional
This arrangement (c) Copyright 1978 Tolka Music

The lark ____ in the morn - ing She ris - es off her

nest, She goes home ___ in the eve - ning with the dew all on her

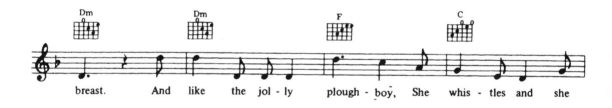

breast. And like the jol - ly plough - boy, She whis - tles and she

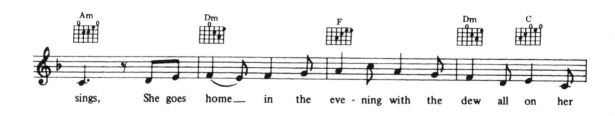

sings, She goes home___ in the eve - ning with the dew all on her

To Coda

(Inst. break 3rd time)

(last time)

Oh Rog - er the plough - boy, he
One eve - ning com - ing home from the
When twen - ty long weeks they were
Here's a health ___ to young plough - boys where-

is a dash - ing blade, He goes whis - tl - ing and sing - ing ov - er
rakes ___ of the town, _____ The mead - ows they are green and the
ov - er and were past _____ Her mam - my chanced to not - ice how she
- ev - er you may be, _____ That likes to have a bon - ny lass a -

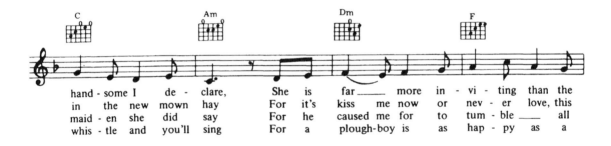

yon - der green blade. He met with pret - ty Su - san, she's
grass it is cut down. If I should chance to tum - ble all
thickened round the waist. It was the hand - some plough - boy the
- sitting on his knee with a jug of good strong port - er, you'll

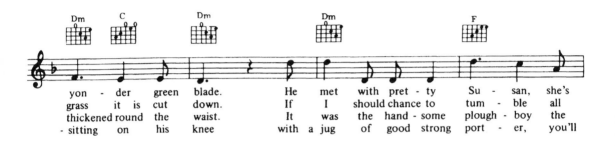

hand - some I de - clare, She is far ___ more in - vi - ting than the
in the new mown hay For it's kiss me now or nev - er love, this
maid - en she did say For he caused me for to tum - ble ___ all
whis - tle and you'll sing For a plough-boy is as hap - py as a

D.S. al Coda

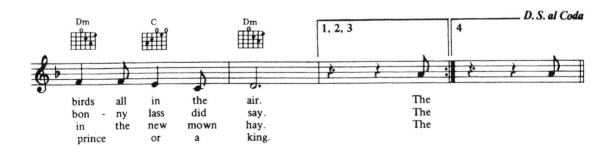

| 1, 2, 3 | 4 |

birds all in the air. The
bon - ny lass did say. The
in the new mown hay. The
prince or a king.

✛ CODA

THE ENNISKILLEN DRAGOON

Traditional
This arrangement (c) Copyright 1978 Tolka Music

Fare thee well En - nis - kil - len, Fare thee well for a

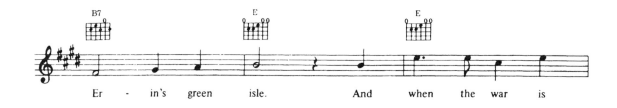

while, And all a - round the bor - ders of

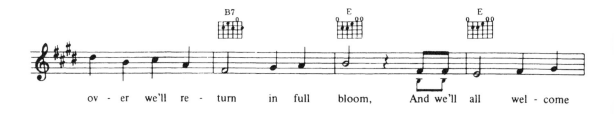

Er - in's green isle. And when the war is

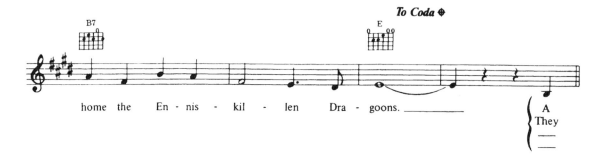

ov - er we'll re - turn in full bloom, And we'll all wel - come

home the En - nis - kil - len Dra - goons. _____

A
They

beau - ti - ful   dam - sel   of   fame   and   re - nown,   A
were   all   dressed   out ___ like ___ gen - tle - men's   sons   Their
Flor - a   dear   Flor - a   your   par - don   I   crave,   It's
Willie   dear - est   Wil - lie   don't   heed   what   they   say   For

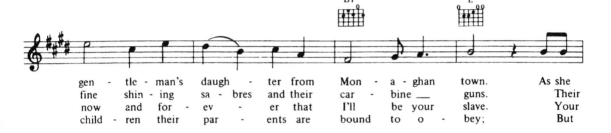

gen - tle - man's   daugh - ter   from   Mon - a - ghan   town.   As she
fine   shin - ing   sa - bres   and their   car - bine ___ guns.   Their
now   and   for - ev - er   that   I'll   be   your   slave.   Your
child - ren   their   par - ents   are   bound   to   o - bey;   But

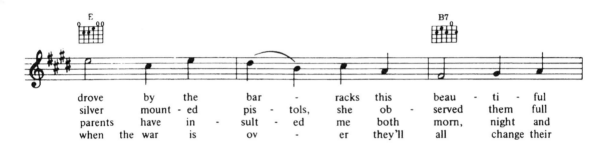

drove   by   the   bar - racks   this   beau - ti - ful
silver   mount - ed   pis - tols,   she   ob - served   them   full
parents   have   in - sult - ed   me   both   morn,   night   and
when   the   war   is   ov - er   they'll   all   change their

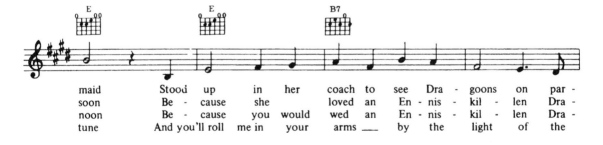

maid   Stood   up   in   her   coach   to   see   Dra - goons   on   par -
soon   Be - cause   she   loved   an   En - nis - kil - len   Dra -
noon   Be - cause   you   would   wed   an   En - nis - kil - len   Dra -
tune   And you'll   roll   me   in   your   arms ___ by   the   light   of   the

D.S. al Coda   **CODA**

ade. _____
goon. _____   }   Fare   thee
goon. _____
moon. _____   ___ Fare   thee

35

THE RISING OF THE MOON

Traditional
This arrangement (c) Copyright 1978 Tolka Music

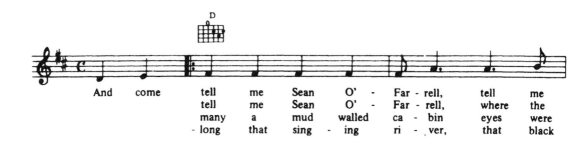

And come tell me Sean O' - Far - rell, tell me
tell me Sean O' - Far - rell, where the
many a mud walled ca - bin eyes were
- long that sing - ing ri - ver, that black

why you hur - ry so, Hush a bhua - chaill, hush and
gather - ing is to be, At the old spot on the
watch - ing through the night, Many a man - ly heart was
mass of men was seen, High a - bove their shin - ing

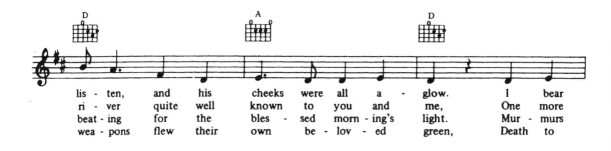

lis - ten, and his cheeks were all a - glow. I bear
ri - ver quite well known to you and me, One more
beat - ing for the bles - sed morn - ing's light. Mur - murs
wea - pons flew their own be - lov - ed green, Death to

or - ders from the cap - tain, get you rea - dy quick and
word for sig - nal to - ken, whis - tle out the march - ing
ran a - long the val - ley to the ban - shee's lone - ly
ev - 'ry foe and trai - tor, whis - tle out the march - ing

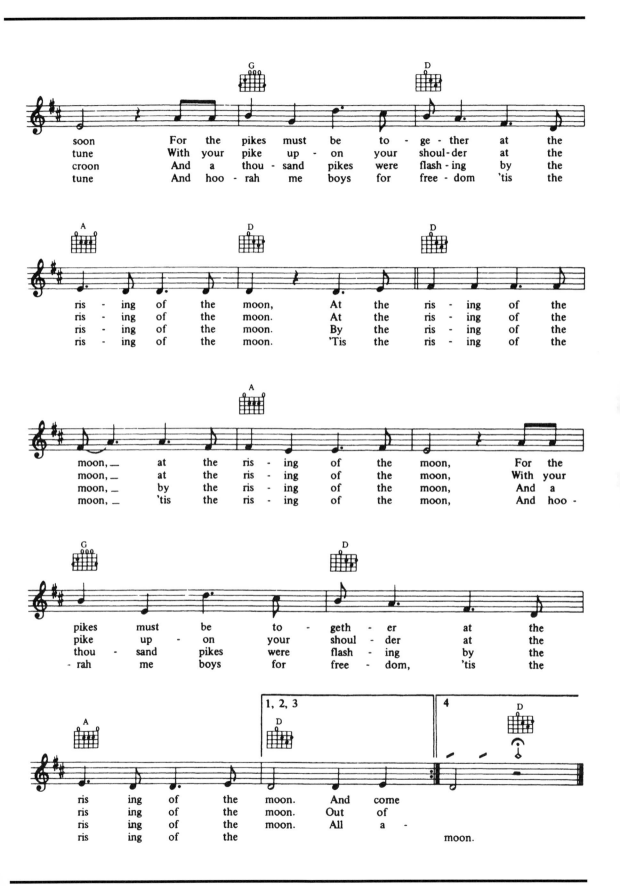

AVONDALE

Traditional
This arrangement (c) Copyright 1978 Tolka Music

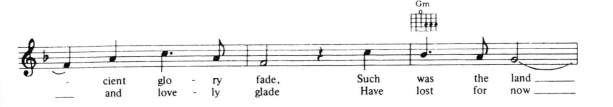

cient glo - ry fade,   Such was the land ____
and love - ly glade   Have lost for now ____

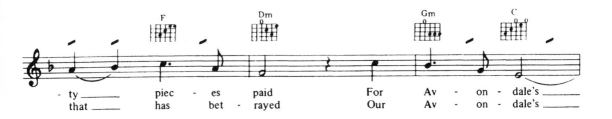

____ where he was laid,   Like Christ was thir -
____ our grand - est Gael,   And cursed the land

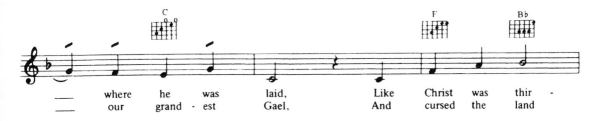

- ty ____ piec - es paid   For Av - on - dale's ____
that ____ has bet - rayed   Our Av - on - dale's

1

____ proud ea - gle.   Oh
____ proud ea - gle.

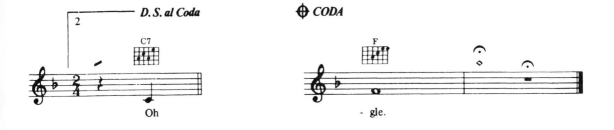

2   *D.S. al Coda*   ⊕ *CODA*

Oh   - gle.

THE UNQUIET GRAVE

Traditional
This arrangement (c) Copyright 1978 Tolka Music

KELLY THE BOY FROM KILLAN

Traditional
This arrangement (c) Copyright 1978 Tolka Music

What's the news, what's the news Oh ___ my bold che - val -
who is the giant with ___ the gold cur - ling
- cor - thy's in flames and ___ old Wex - ford has
gold sun of free - dom ___ grew dark in that

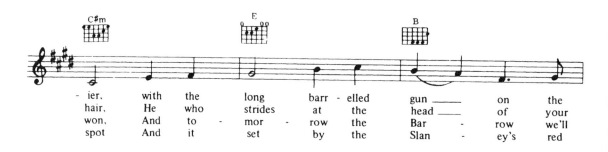

- ier, with the long barr - elled gun ___ on the
hair, He who strides at the head ___ of your
won, And to - mor - row the Bar - row we'll
spot And it set by the Slan - ey's red

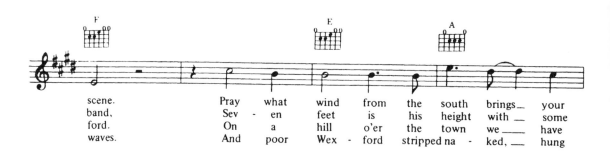

scene. Pray what wind from the south brings ___ your
band, Sev - en feet is his height with ___ some
ford. On a hill o'er the town we ___ have
waves. And poor Wex - ford stripped na - ked, ___ hung

mes - sen - ger here With his hymn of the
in - ches to spare, He ___ looks like a
plant - ed a gun That will bat - ter a
high on a cross With her heart pierced by

dawn _____ for the free.
king _____ in com - mand.
gate - way to Ross.
trait - ors and knaves.

Good - ly
Ah me
All the
Glo - ry -

news, good - ly news do I bring you per -
boys that's the pride of the bold che - val -
pike - men and bargee men will march o'er the
- o glo - ry - o to the brave men who

- force, Good - ly news do I bring bar - gee man,
- iers. The great - est of he - roes and men,
hill, With brave Har - vey to lead in the van,
died For the cause of long down - trod - den man,

For the boys march at dawn from the
So fling your beav - ers a - loft and give
But the fore - most of all in that
Glo - ry - o to Mount Lein - ster's own

south to the north Led by Kel - ly _____ the
three ring - ing cheers For John Kel - ly _____ the
grim gap of death Will be Kel - ly _____ the
dar - ling and pride John _____ Kel - ly _____ the

1, 2, 3

4

boy _____ from Kil - lan.
boy _____ from Kil - lan.
boy _____ from Kil - lan.
boy _____ from Kil - lan.

Tell me
En - nis -
But the

FOUR GREEN FIELDS

Words and music by Tommy Makem
(c) Copyright 1978 Keady Music

THE TOWN I LOVED SO WELL

Words and music by P Coulter and B Martin
(c) Copyright 1973 Mews Music Limited

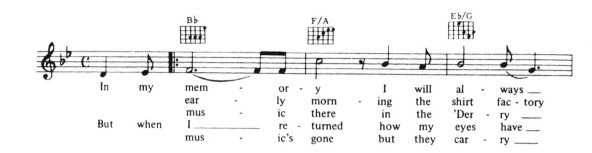

	Bb	F/A	Eb/G
In my	mem - or - y	I will al - ways
	ear - ly morn - ing	the shirt fac - tory
	mus - ic there	in the 'Der - ry
But when I	re - turned	how my eyes have
	mus - ic's gone	but they car - ry

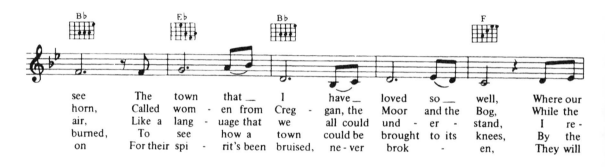

Bb	Eb	Bb	F
see	The town that I	have loved so well,	Where our
horn,	Called wom - en from Creg - gan, the	Moor and the Bog,	While the
air,	Like a lang - uage that we	all could und - er - stand,	I re -
burned,	To see how a town	could be brought to its knees,	By the
on	For their spi - rit's been bruised,	ne - ver brok - en,	They will

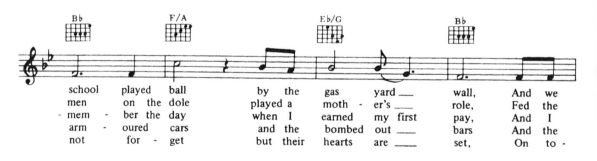

Bb	F/A	Eb/G	Bb
school	played ball	by the gas yard	wall,	And we
men	on the dole	played a moth - er's	role,	Fed the
- mem - ber the day	when I	earned my first	pay,	And I
arm - oured cars	and the	bombed out	bars	And the
not for - get	but their	hearts are	set,	On to -

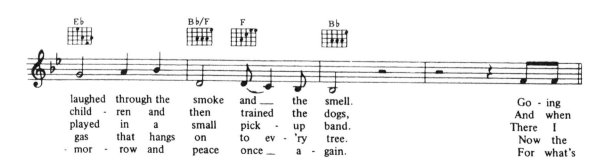

Eb	Bb/F	F	Bb
laughed through the	smoke and the	smell.		Go - ing
child - ren and	then trained the	dogs,		And when
played in a	small pick - up	band.		There I
gas that hangs on	to ev - 'ry	tree.		Now the
- mor - row and	peace once a -	gain.		For what's

FALSE HEARTED LOVER

Traditional
This arrangement (c) Copyright 1978 Tolka Music

I once loved a maid and I loved her so ___ well,
I saw my love to the church ___ go,
I saw my love sit down to ___ dine,
boys of the forest they ask it of ___ me
dig me a grave I let ye dig it so ___ deep

That I hat-ed all oth-ers Who spoke of her ill, And
With her maids and bride-maid-ens She made a fine show, And
Well I sat down be-side her, I poured out her wine, And I
How man-y straw-berr-ies Grow in the salt sea, And I
And cov-er it ov-er With flow-ers so sweet, And

now she's re-ward-ed me well for my pains, For she's gone to be
I foll-owed on with my heart full of woe, For she's to be
drank to the girl that should have been mine, But she was now
ask it them back with a tear in my eye, How man-y ships
close my poor eye-lids for-ev-er in sleep And may-be in

1, 2, 3, 4

wed to an-oth-er. _____
wed to an-oth-er. _____
wed to an-oth-er. _____
sail in the for-est. _____
death I'll for-get her. _____

2. When
3. Then
4. The
5. Go

5

rall.